HOW TO PRAY
BOOK FOR MUSLIM KIDS
95 pages and 8 x 10 in

This book belongs to:

....

....

....

Three chapters:

FIRST CHAPTER:

Prayer
in
ISLAM

Complete Salah

From page n° 3 till page n° 64

بِاسْمِ اللهِ الرحمانِ الرحيمِ

« Bismi llaahi rrahmaani rrahiime »

In the name of Allah, Most Gracious, Most Merciful.

FIRST OF ALL:

If you want to pray, you should keep yourself in state
of clean and pure. And so as to be so,
you have to perform ablution.

"Prayer without ablution is invalid »

The five daily prayers

PRAYERS	RAKAAHS	RECITATION	TIME OF THE PRAYERS
ALFAJR	2 Rakaahs	Recite aloud	Dawn, before sunrise
ADDUHER	4 Rakaahs	Recite silently	midday, after the sun passes its highest
AL-AASER	4 Rakaahs	Recite silently	The late part of the afternoon
ALMAGHEB	3 Rakaahs	The first and the second «rakaah»: recite aloud; the third «rakaah» : recite silently.	Just after sunset
AL-AISHA	4 Rakaahs	The first and the second «rakaah»: recite aloud; the third and the fourth «rakaah»: recite silently	Between sunset and midnight

Of course, muslim women/girls have to recite all quranic verses silently while performing the prayers.

We will give you an illustration of praying
in Islam with images, and we will take
as an example the prayer of « AL-AASER »
with four silent « RAKAAH ».

So, the presentation will be step by step so
as all kids and even adults can understand
and can perfom the prayer of « AL-AASER »
easily and fluently.

So, let's start.

بإسم الله الرحمان الرحيم
« Bismi llaahi rrahmaani rrahiime »
In the name of Allah, Most Gracious, Most Merciful.

This is the illustration of the first « RAKAAH »

First, stand up, your face towards QIBLA, MECCA

Then, always start with « bismillaah »: in the name of Allah.

You should have the intention to pray and then say:

الله أكبر الله أكبر

«Allaahou akbar, allaahou akbar.»

Allah is Great, Allah is Great

أشهد أن لا إلاه إلا الله

« ashehadou anna laa ilaaha illa llaah »

I bear witness that there is no god but Allah

وأشهد أن محمدا عبده و رسوله

« wa ashehadou anna mohammadane abdouhou
 wa rassoulouhou »

**And I bear witness that Muhammad is His slave
and Prophet**

حي على الصلاة حي على الفلاح

« hayya alaa ssalaati, hayya halaa lfalaahi »

Come to prayer, come to success

قد قامت الصلاة

«qade qaamati ssalaatou»

 Prayer has been established,

الله أكبر الله أكبر

«allaahou akbar , allaahou akbar. »

Allah is Great, Allah is Great

لا إلاه إلا الله

« laa ilaaha illa llaah »

there is no god but Allah.

Then, start your prayer by saying:

الله أكبر

« Allaahou akbar »

Allah is Great

- Look at the following image -

الله أكبر
Allah is Great
« allaahou akbar »

Then, recite silently Surah Al-Fatiha: Verse 2

بِإِسم الله الرحمان الرحيم
« Bismillaahi rrahmaani rrahiime »
In the name of Allah, Most Gracious, Most Merciful.

الْحَمْدُ لِلَّهِ رَبِّ الْعَالَمِينَ
« alhamdou lillaahi rabbi al-aalamiina »
Praise be to Allah, the Cherisher and Sustainer of the worlds,

الرَّحْمَٰنِ الرَّحِيمِ
« arrahmaani rrahiime »
Most Gracious, Most Merciful,

مَالِكِ يَوْمِ الدِّينِ
« maaliki yawemi ddiine »
Master of the Day of Judgment.

إِيَّاكَ نَعْبُدُ وَإِيَّاكَ نَسْتَعِينُ
« iyyaaka na-aaboudo wa iyyaaka nasta-aaiine »
Thee do we worship, and Thine aid we seek.

اهْدِنَا الصِّرَاطَ الْمُسْتَقِيمَ
« ihdina ssiraata almoustaqiime »
 Show us the straight way,

»صِرَاطَ الَّذِينَ أَنْعَمْتَ عَلَيْهِمْ غَيْرِ الْمَغْضُوبِ عَلَيْهِمْ وَلَا الضَّالِّينَ. امين.
 « siraata lladiina ane-aameta aalayehime, ghayri almaghdoubi
 aalayehime, wala ddaliine. Amiiiiine »
 The way of those on whom Thou hast bestowed Thy Grace,
those whose (portion) is not wrath, and who go not astray.
Amine.

After finishing Surah ALFATIHA, recite silently any verse from the Quran:
For example: Surah AL IKHLAS

باسم الله الرحمن الرحيم

« Bismillaahi rrahmaani rrahiime »

In the Name of Allâh, the Most Beneficent, the Most Merciful.

قُلْ هُوَ اللَّهُ أَحَدٌ

« qoul houa llaahou ahade »

Say "Allâh is (the) One

اللَّهُ الصَّمَدُ

« allaahou ssamade »

The Self-Sufficient Master

لَمْ يَلِدْ وَلَمْ يُولَدْ

« lame yalide walame youlade »

"He begets not, nor was He begotten.

وَلَمْ يَكُنْ لَهُ كُفُوًا أَحَدٌ

« walame yakoune lahou koufou-ane ahade »

And there is none co-equal or comparable unto Him.

Then, say: :

الله أكبر

« Allaahou akbar »

Allah is Great

And, do as in the following image:

Then, say three times :

"Subhaana rabiyya al-aaddiime » :

سبحان ربي العظيم

Glory be to my God

Then, standing upright again and saying:

"Sami-aa llaahou liman hamidah" سمع الله لمن حمده

« Allah listens to those who praise Him »

« Rabbanaa walaka lhamd » ربنا و لك الحمد

Praise be to our God

<u>Then, say</u>: :

الله أكبر

« Allaahou akbar »

Allah is Great

الله أكبر
Allah is Great
« allaahou akbar »

While prostrating, you have to say 3 times :

"Subhaana rabiyya al-aalaa"

سبحان ربي الأعلى

Glory to my God

Raising the head and saying:

"Allaahou akbar"

الله أكبر

Allah is Great

Then, say a request such as :

اللهم إغفر لي و إرحمني

« Allaahoumaa ighfir lii wa rhamnii »

My God, forgive me and have mercy on me

Then slowly bending down to prostrate and saying:

"Allaahou akbar"

الله أكبر

Allah is Great

Once again, while prostrating you have to say 3 times :

"Subhaana rabiyya al-aalaa"

سبحان ربي الأعلى

Glory to my God

THE SECOND « RAKAAH »

This is the illustration of the second « RAKAAH »

Then, stand up again, your face towards the QIBLA, MECCA

Then, start your second RAKAAH by saying:

الله أكبر

« Allaahou akbar »

Allah is Great

- Look at the following image -

الله أكبر
Allah is Great
« allaahou akbar »

Then, recite once again silently Surah Al-Fatiha: Verse 2

بِإِسم الله الرحمان الرحيم
« Bismillaahi rrahmaani rrahiime »
In the name of Allah, Most Gracious, Most Merciful.

الْحَمْدُ لِلَّهِ رَبِّ الْعَالَمِينَ
« alhamdou lillaahi rabbi al-aalamiine »
Praise be to Allah, the Cherisher and Sustainer of the worlds,

الرَّحْمَٰنِ الرَّحِيمِ
« arrahmaani rrahiime »
Most Gracious, Most Merciful,

مَالِكِ يَوْمِ الدِّينِ
« maaliki yawemi ddiine »
Master of the Day of Judgment.

إِيَّاكَ نَعْبُدُ وَإِيَّاكَ نَسْتَعِينُ
« iyyaaka na-aaboudo wa iyyaaka nasta-aaiine »
Thee do we worship, and Thine aid we seek.

اهْدِنَا الصِّرَاطَ الْمُسْتَقِيمَ
« ihdina ssiraata almoustaqiime »
Show us the straight way,

»صِرَاطَ الَّذِينَ أَنْعَمْتَ عَلَيْهِمْ غَيْرِ الْمَغْضُوبِ عَلَيْهِمْ وَلَا الضَّالِّينَ. امين.
« siraata lladina ane-aameta aalayehime, ghayri almaghdoubi
aalayehime, wala ddaliine. Amiiiiine »
The way of those on whom Thou hast bestowed Thy Grace, those whose (portion) is not wrath, and who go not astray. Amine.

After finishing surah ALFATIHA, recite silently any verse from the Quran:
For example: سورة النصر *Surah An-Nasr:*

باسم الله الرحمن الرحيم

« Bismillaahi rrahmaani rrahiime »

In the Name of Allâh, the Most Beneficent, the Most Merciful.

إِذَا جَاءَ نَصْرُ اللَّهِ وَالْفَتْحُ

« idaa jaa a nasrou llaahi walfatehou »

When comes the Help of Allah, and Victory,

وَرَأَيْتَ النَّاسَ يَدْخُلُونَ فِي دِينِ اللَّهِ أَفْوَاجًا

« wa ra-ayeta nnaasa yadkhoulouna fii diini
llaahi afwaajane »

**And thou dost see the people enter
Allah's Religion in crowds,**

فَسَبِّحْ بِحَمْدِ رَبِّكَ وَاسْتَغْفِرْهُ إِنَّهُ كَانَ تَوَّابًا

« fasabbih bismi rabbika wa staghfirhou innahou kaana
tawaabane »

**Celebrate the praises of thy Lord, and pray for His
Forgiveness: For He is Oft-Returning (in Grace and
Mercy).**

Then, say: :

الله أكبر

« Allaahou akbar »

Allah is Great

And, do as in the following image:

Then, say three times :

"Subhaana rabiyya al-aaddiime » :

سبحان ربي العظيم

Glory be to my God

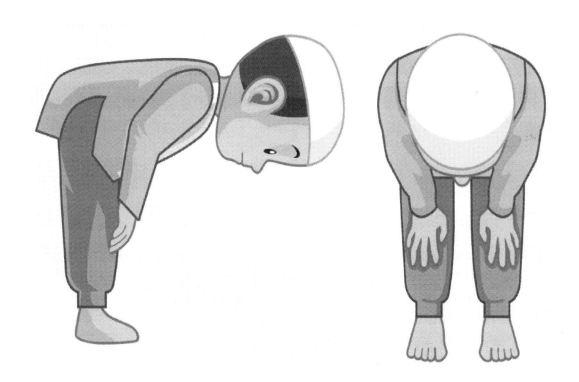

Then, standing upright again and saying:

"Sami-aa llaahou limane hamidah" سمع الله لمن حمده

« Allah listens to those who praise Him »

« Rabbanaa walaka lhamd » ربنا و لك الحمد

Praise be to our God

Then, say: :

الله أكبر

« Allaahou akbar »

Allah is Great

While prostrating, you have to say three times :

"Subhaana rabiyya al-aalaa"

سبحان ربي الأعلى

Glory to my God

Raising the head and saying:

"Allaahou akbar"

الله أكبر

Allah is Great

Then, say a request such as :

اللهم إغفر لي و إرحمني

« Allaahoumma ighfir lii wa rhamenii »

My God, forgive me and have mercy on me

Then slowly bending down to prostrate and saying:

"Allaahou akbar"

الله أكبر

Allah is Great

Once again, while prostrating you have to say 3 times :

"Subhaana rabiyya al-aalaa"

سبحان ربي الأعلى

Glory to my God

Raising the head and saying:

"Allaahou akbar"

الله أكبر

Allah is Great

الله أكبر
Allah is Great
« allaahou akbar »

Then, you sit on your knees to recite the tashahhud while moving your finger of your right hand:

التحيات لله و الصلوات و الطيبات،

« Attahiyaatou lillaah wa ssalawaatou wa ttayibaate »

All compliments, prayers and pure words are due to Allaah.

السلام عليك أيها النبي ، و رحمة الله و بركاته

«assalaamou aalayeka ayouha nnabii warahmatou llaahi wa barakaatouhou »

Peace be upon you, O Prophet, and the mercy of Allaah and His blessings.

السلام علينا و على عباد الله الصالحين،

« assalaamou aalayenaa wa aalaa aibaadi llahi ssaalihiina »

Peace be upon us and upon the righteous slaves of Allaah.

أشهد أن لا إله إلا الله،

« ashehadou anna laa ilaaha illa llaah »

I bear witness that there is no god except Allaah

و أشهد أن محمدا عبده و رسوله.

«wa ashehadou anna mouhammadane aabedouhou wa rasoulouhou »

and I bear witness that Muhammad is His slave and Messenger

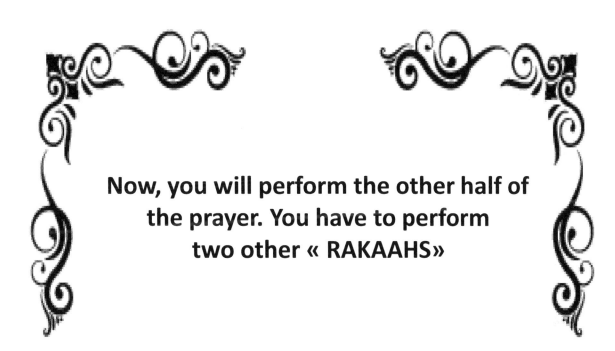

Now, you will perform the other half of the prayer. You have to perform two other « RAKAAHS»

THE THIRD RAKAAH

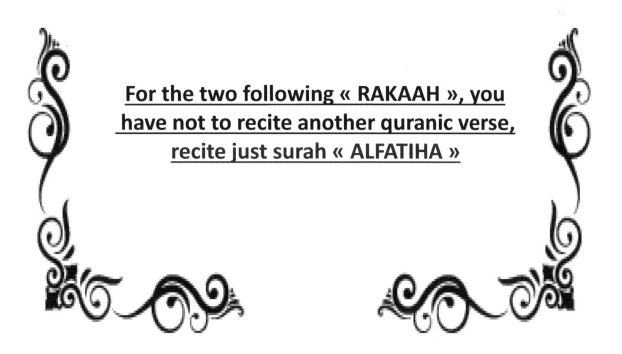

For the two following « RAKAAH », you have not to recite another quranic verse, recite just surah « ALFATIHA »

This is the illustration of the third « RAKAAH »

Then, start your third « RAKAAH» by saying:

الله أكبر

« Allaahou akbar »

Allah is Great

- Look at the following image -

Then, recite again silently surah Al-Fatiha:

بإسم الله الرحمان الرحيم
« Bismillaahi rrahmaani rrahiime »
In the name of Allah, Most Gracious, Most Merciful.

الْحَمْدُ لِلَّهِ رَبِّ الْعَالَمِينَ
« alhamdou lilaahi rabbi al-aalamiine »
Praise be to Allah, the Cherisher and Sustainer of the worlds,

الرَّحْمَٰنِ الرَّحِيمِ
« arrahmaani rrahiime »
Most Gracious, Most Merciful,

مَالِكِ يَوْمِ الدِّينِ
« maaliki yawemi ddiine »
Master of the Day of Judgment.

إِيَّاكَ نَعْبُدُ وَإِيَّاكَ نَسْتَعِينُ
« iyyaaka na-aaboudo wa iyyaaka nasta-aaiine »
Thee do we worship, and Thine aid we seek.

اهْدِنَا الصِّرَاطَ الْمُسْتَقِيمَ
« ihdina ssiraata almoustaqiime »
Show us the straight way,

«صِرَاطَ الَّذِينَ أَنْعَمْتَ عَلَيْهِمْ غَيْرِ الْمَغْضُوبِ عَلَيْهِمْ وَلَا الضَّالِّينَ. امين.
« siraata lladina ane-aameta aalayehime, ghayri almaghdoubi
aalayehime, wala ddaliine. Amiiiiine »
**The way of those on whom Thou hast bestowed Thy Grace,
those whose (portion) is not wrath, and who go not astray.
Amine.**

<u>Then, say: :</u>

الله أكبر

« Allaahou akbar »

Allah is Great

الله أكبر
Allah is Great
« allaahou akbar »

And, do as in the following image:

Then, say three times :

"Subhaana rabiyya al-aaddiime » :

سبحان ربي العظيم

Glory be to my God

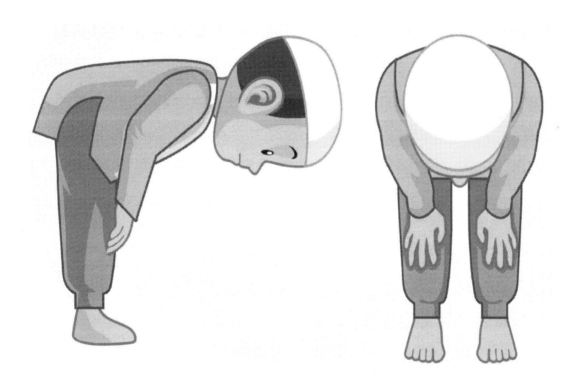

Then, standing upright again and saying:

"Sami-aa llaahou liman hamidah" سمع الله لمن حمده

« Allah listens to those who praise Him »

« Rabbanaa walaka lhamd » ربنا و لك الحمد

Praise be to our God

Then, say:

الله أكبر

« Allaahou akbar »

Allah is Great

While prostrating, you have to say 3 times :

"Subhaana rabiyya al-aalaa"

سبحان ربي الأعلى

Glory to my God

Raising the head and saying:

"Allaahou akbar"

الله أكبر

Allah is Great

الله أكبر
Allah is Great
« allaahou akbar »

Then, say a request such as :

اللهم إغفر لي و إرحمني

« Allaahouma ighfir lii wa rhamnii »

My God, forgive me and have mercy on me

Then slowly bending down to prostrate and saying:

"Allaahou akbar"

الله أكبر

Allah is Great

الله أكبر
Allah is Great
« allaahou akbar »

Once again, while prostrating you have to say 3 times :

"Subhaana rabiyya al-aalaa"

سبحان ربي الأعلى

Glory to my God

FOURTH RAKAAH

This is the illustration of the fourth « RAKAAH »

Then, start your fourth « RAKAAH» by saying:

الله أكبر

« Allaahou akbar »

Allah is Great

- Look at the following image -

Then, recite once again surah Al-Fatiha: Verse 2

بإسم الله الرحمان الرحيم
« Bismillaahi rrahmaani rrahiime »
In the name of Allah, Most Gracious, Most Merciful.

الْحَمْدُ لِلَّهِ رَبِّ الْعَالَمِينَ
« alhamdou lilaahi rabbi al-aalamiine »
Praise be to Allah, the Cherisher and Sustainer of the worlds,

الرَّحْمَٰنِ الرَّحِيمِ
« arrahmaani rrahiime »
Most Gracious, Most Merciful,

مَالِكِ يَوْمِ الدِّينِ
« maaliki yawemi ddiine »
Master of the Day of Judgment.

إِيَّاكَ نَعْبُدُ وَإِيَّاكَ نَسْتَعِينُ
« iyyaaka na-aaboudo wa iyyaaka nasta-aaiine »
Thee do we worship, and Thine aid we seek.

اهْدِنَا الصِّرَاطَ الْمُسْتَقِيمَ
« ihdinaa ssiraata almoustaqiime »
Show us the straight way,

»صِرَاطَ الَّذِينَ أَنْعَمْتَ عَلَيْهِمْ غَيْرِ الْمَغْضُوبِ عَلَيْهِمْ وَلَا الضَّالِّينَ. امين.
« siraata lladina ane-aameta aalayehime, ghayri almaghdoubi aalayehime, wala ddaliine. Amiiiiine »
The way of those on whom Thou hast bestowed Thy Grace, those whose (portion) is not wrath, and who go not astray. Amine.

Then, say: :

الله أكبر

« Allaahou akbar »

Allah is Great

And, do as in the following image:

Then, say three times :

"Subhaana rabiyya al-aaddiime » :

سبحان ربي العظيم

Glory be to my God

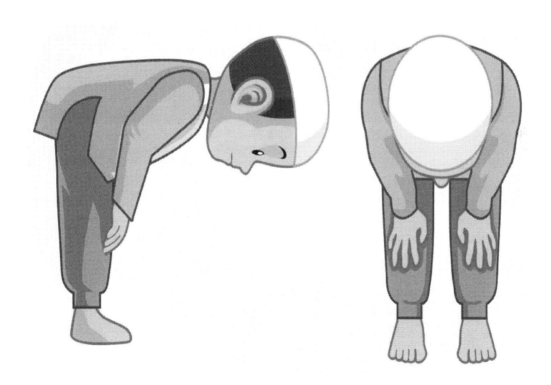

Then, standing upright again and saying:

"Sami-aa llaahou limane hamidah" سمع الله لمن حمده

« Allah listens to those who praise Him »

« Rabbanaa walaka lhamd » ربنا و لك الحمد

Praise be to our God

Then, say: :

الله أكبر

« Allaahou akbar »

Allah is Great

While prostrating, you have to say 3 times :

"Subhaana rabiyya al-aalaa"

سبحان ربي الأعلى

Glory to my God

Raising the head and saying:

"Allaahou akbar"

الله أكبر

Allah is Great

Then, say a request such as :

اللهم إغفر لي و إرحمني

« Allaahouma ighfir lii wa rhamnii »

My God, forgive me and have mercy on me

Then slowly bending down to prostrate and saying:

"Allaahou akbar"

الله أكبر

Allah is Great

Once again, while prostrating you have to say 3 times :

"Subhaana rabiyya al-aalaa"

سبحان ربي الأعلى

Glory to my God

Raising the head and saying:

"Allaahou akbar"

الله أكبر

Allah is Great

الله أكبر
Allah is Great
« allaahou akbar »

Then, you sit on your knees to recite the tashahhud
and Ibrahimya prayer, while moving your finger
of your right hand:
(as written on the following page)

The Tashahhud and Ibrahimya prayer:

التحيات لله و الصلوات و الطيبات،

« Attahiyaatou lillaah wa ssalawaatou wa ttayibaate »

All compliments, prayers and pure words are due to Allaah.

السلام عليك أيها النبي ، و رحمة الله و بركاته

«assalaamou aalayeka ayouha nnabii warahmatou llaahi wa barakaatouhou »

Peace be upon you, O Prophet, and the mercy of Allaah and His blessings.

السلام علينا و على عباد الله الصالحين،

« assalaamou aalayenaa wa aalaa aibaadi llaahi ssaalihiina »

Peace be upon us and upon the righteous slaves of Allaah.

أشهد أن لا إله إلا الله،

« ashehadou anna laa ilaaha illa llaah »

I bear witness that there is no god except Allaah

و أشهد أن محمدا عبده و رسوله.

«wa ashehadou anna mouhammadane aabedouhou wa rasoulouhou »

and I bear witness that Muhammad is His slave and Messenger.

اللهم صلي على محمد و على آل محمد

« allahoumma salli aalaa mouhammadine wa aalaa aali mouhammadine »

O Allaah, send prayers upon Muhammad and upon the family of Muhammad,

كما صليت على إبراهيم و على آل إبراهيم

« kamaa sallayeta aalaa ibrahiim wa aalaa aali ibrahiim »

as You sent prayers upon Ibraaheem and the family of Ibraaheem

وبارك على محمد و على آل محمد

« wa baarik aalaa mouhammadine wa aalaa aali mouhammadine »

O Allaah, bless Muhammad and the family of Muhammad

كما باركت على إبراهيم و على آل إبراهيم

« kamaa baarakta aalaa ibrahiim wa aalaa aali ibrahiim »

as You blessed Ibraaheem and the family of Ibraaheem,

في العالمين إنك حميد مجيد.

« fii l aalamiina innaka hamiidoune majiide »

You are indeed Worthy of Praise, Full of Glory.

The termination of the prayers takes place as follows:

The head is turned to the right and you say:

"Assalaamou aalaykoum wa rahmatou llaahi ta-aalaa wa barakaatouh"

السلام عليكم و رحمة الله تعالى و بركاته

Peace, mercy and blessings of Almighty God

Then the head is turned to the left and you say:

"Assalaamou aalaykoum wa rahmatou llaahi
ta-aalaa wa barakaatouh"

السلام عليكم و رحمة الله تعالى و بركاته

Peace, mercy and blessings of Almighty God

The five daily prayers recapitulation

Prayers	Composition of each prayer
Al-Fajr	Two loudly Rakaahs + Tashahhud + Ibrahimya Prayer + Salam Aalyekoume
Adduher	Two silent Rakaahs + Tashahhud + Two silent Rakaahs + Tashahhud + Ibrahimya Prayer + Salam Aalyekoume
Al-Aaser	Two silent Rakaahs + Tashahhud + Two silent Rakaahs + Tashahhud + Ibrahimya Prayer + Salam Aalyekoume
Al-Maghreb	Two loudly Rakaahs + Tashahhud + One silent Rakkah + Tashahhud + Ibrahimya Prayer + Salam Aalyekoume
Al-Aishaa	Two loudly Rakaahs + Tashahhud + Two silent Rakaahs + Tashahhud + Ibrahimya Prayer + Salam Aalyekoume

Once again, it's very important to mention that **girls** have to recite Quran **silently** during all their prayers.

SECOND CHAPTER:

ABLUTION
In
ISLAM

From page n° 65 till page n° 79

ABLUTION IN ISLAM

Of course, if you want to pray, you should keep yourself in state of clean and pure. And so as to be so, you have to perform ablution.
"Prayer without ablution is invalid »

Indeed, ablution « ALWOUDOU » is an islamic procedure for cleansing the whole body or parts of it. The ablution is normally done in preparation for formal daily five obligatory prayers or before handling and reading the Quran.

There are three types of ablution:

1/ Partial ablution: washing parts of the body using water. This type of ablution is an acte for purifying some activities such as urination, defecation, flatulence, deep sleep, light bleeding. This ablution is perfomed everyday.

2/ Dry ablution: « Attayamoume »: replacing water with stone or sand when there is no water.

3/ Full ablution: washing the whole body using water after sexual intercourse, childbirth or menstruation. This involves similar steps to the above (1rst ablution), with the addition of rinsing the left and right sides of the body as well.

In this part of this book, we will present for you how you can perfom islamic partial ablution step by step so as to practice your daily prayers correctly.

So, when someone determines to cleanse oneself for prayer, for the sake of Allah. Then, one begins with :

بِإِسْمِ اللهِ الرَّحْمَانِ الرَّحِيمِ
« bismi llaahi rrahmaani rrahiime »
<u>In the name of Allah, Most Gracious,</u>
<u>Most Merciful.</u>

And with water, one then begins to wash some parts of one's body as follows:

:

بإسم الله الرحمان الرحيم
« Bismi llaahi rrahmaani rrahiime »
<u>In the name of Allah, Most Gracious,</u>
<u>Most Merciful.</u>

1/ The hands:

Wash the hands three times, making sure that the water reaches between the fingers and all over the hands up to the wrist

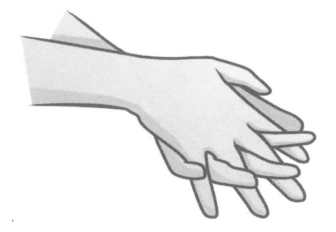

2/ The mouth:

Wash the mouth three times, bringing a handful of water to the mouth and rinsing thoroughly.

3/ The noses

Wash the nose three times, using the right hand to bring water up to the nose, sniffing the water, and using the left hand to expel it.

4/ The face:

Wash the face three times, from the forehead to the chin and from ear to ear.

5/ The arms:

Wash the arms three times, up to the elbows, starting with the right arm.

First, the right arm.

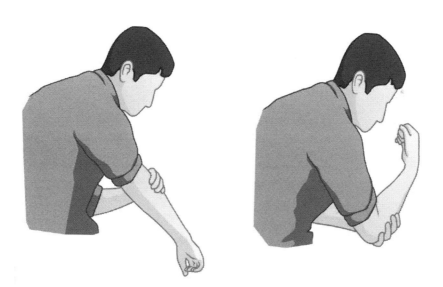

Then, the left arm.

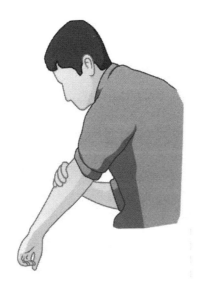
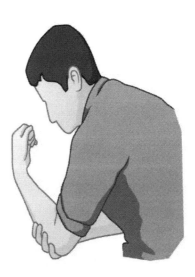

6/ The head:

Wash the head one time, using wet hands to wipe over the head from front to back and front again.

7/ The ears:

Wash the ears one time, using wet fingers to wipe the inside and outside of the ears.

8/ The feet:

Wash the feet three times, up to the ankles, starting with the right.

So, first the right foot.

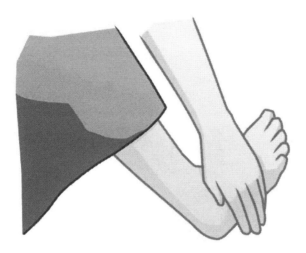

Then, wash the left foot.

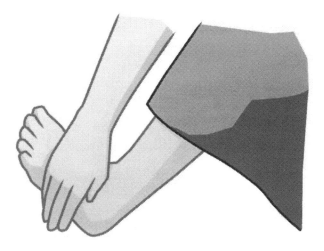

It's very important to mention that
before each everyday prayer,
the muslim person does not need
to repeat the ablution « al woudou »
if it is not broken.

* * * * *

And the actions that may break
the ablution include:
- Urination,
- Defecation,
- Flatulence,
- Deep sleep,
Falling unconscious,
Bleeding from a wound.

Of course, after each urination or each
defecation, the parts involved are to be
washed before performing the ablution..

THIRD CHAPTER:

DUA
From Quran

From page n° 80 till page n° 95

Now, we will present for you some DUAs
from the Quran. Indeed, these Duas
are quranic verses. And you can
use them during your prayers or after
performing them. You can also use them
whenever you want.

So, let's start.

بإسم الله الرحمان الرحيم
« Bismi llaahi rrahmaani rrahiime »
In the name of Allah, Most Gracious, Most Merciful.

بسم الله الرحمن الرحيم
« bismillahi rrahmani rrahime »
In the Name of Allâh, the Most Beneficent, the Most Merciful.

سورة الحشر : Surah *Al-Hashr (Ayaa 10)*

" رَبَّنَا اغْفِرْ لَنَا وَلِإِخْوَانِنَا الَّذِينَ سَبَقُونَا بِالْإِيمَانِ وَلَا تَجْعَلْ فِي قُلُوبِنَا غِلًّا لِلَّذِينَ آمَنُوا رَبَّنَا إِنَّكَ رَءُوفٌ رَحِيمٌ. "

« Rabbanaa ghfire lanaa wa li-ikhwaaninaa lladiina sabaqounaa bil-iimaani, wa laa tajaale fii qouloubinaa ghillane lilladiina aamanou, rabbanaa innaka ra-oufoune rahiimoune. »

« Our Lord. Forgive us, and our brethren who came before us into the Faith, and leave not, in our hearts, rancour against those who have believed. Our Lord! Thou art indeed Full of Kindness, Most Merciful. »

Surah Nooh (Ayaa 28) : سورة نوح

رَبِّ اغْفِرْ لِي وَلِوَالِدَيَّ وَلِمَنْ دَخَلَ بَيْتِيَ مُؤْمِنًا وَلِلْمُؤْمِنِينَ وَالْمُؤْمِنَاتِ وَلَا تَزِدِ الظَّالِمِينَ إِلَّا تَبَارًا

« Rabbi ghfire lii wa li-waalidayya wa limane dakhala bayetii mou-minane , wa lilmou-miniina wa lmou-minaati, wa laa tazidi ddalimiina illaa tabarane. »

« My Lord. Forgive me, and my parents, and him who enters my home as a believer, and all the believing men and women. And to the Zâlimûn (polytheists, wrong-doers, and disbelievers) grant You no increase but destruction. »

سورة الممتحنة : **Surah AL Mumtahina**

رَبَّنَا عَلَيْكَ تَوَكَّلْنَا وَإِلَيْكَ أَنَبْنَا وَإِلَيْكَ الْمَصِيرُ (4)

« Rabbanaa aalayeka tawakkalnaa wa ilayeka anabnaa wa ilayeka lmasiirou »

« Our Lord. in Thee do we trust, and to Thee do we turn in repentance: to Thee is Final Goal. »

Surah AL Mumtahina : سورة الممتحنة

رَبَّنَا لَا تَجْعَلْنَا فِتْنَةً لِلَّذِينَ كَفَرُوا وَاغْفِرْ لَنَا رَبَّنَا إِنَّكَ أَنْتَ الْعَزِيزُ الْحَكِيمُ (5)

« Rabbanaa laa taj-aalnaa fitnatane lilladiina kafarou wa ghfire lanaa, rabbanaa innaka aneta l-aazizou lhakimou.»

"Our Lord. Make us not a trial for the Unbelievers, but forgive us, our Lord. for Thou art the Exalted in Might, the Wise."

سورة الدخان : Sura Ad-Dukhaan (Ayaa 12)

رَبَّنَا اكْشِفْ عَنَّا الْعَذَابَ إِنَّا مُؤْمِنُونَ

« Rabbanaa kshif aannaa l-aadaaba
innaa mou-minouna. »

"Our Lord. Remove the torment from us, really we shall become believers."

Surah Surah Yunus :سورة يونس

فَقَالُوا عَلَى اللَّهِ تَوَكَّلْنَا رَبَّنَا لَا تَجْعَلْنَا فِتْنَةً لِلْقَوْمِ الظَّالِمِينَ (85)

« Faqaalou aalaa llaahi tawakkalnaa, rabbanaa laa taj-aalnaa fitnatane lilqawemi ddalimiina »

« They said: In Allâh we put our trust. Our Lord. Make us not a trial for the folk who are Zâlimûn (polytheists and wrong-doers).»

Surah Surah Yunus :سورة يونس

وَنَجِّنَا بِرَحْمَتِكَ مِنَ الْقَوْمِ الْكَافِرِينَ (86)

« Wa najjinaa bi-rahmatika mina lqawemi lkaafiriina. »

« And save us by Your Mercy from the disbelieving folk. »

Surah At-Tawba : سورة التوبة

حَسْبُنَا اللَّهُ سَيُؤْتِينَا اللَّهُ مِنْ فَضْلِهِ وَرَسُولُهُ إِنَّا إِلَى اللَّهِ رَاغِبُون (59)

« Hasbouna llaahou sayoutiinaa llaahou mine fadlihi wa rasoulouhou, innaa ilaa llaahi raaghibouna »

« Allâh is Sufficient for us. Allâh will give us of His Bounty, and so will His Messenger. We implore Allâh. »

سورة التوبة : **Surah At-Tawba**

حَسْبِيَ اللَّهُ لَا إِلَهَ إِلَّا هُوَ عَلَيْهِ تَوَكَّلْتُ وَهُوَ رَبُّ الْعَرْشِ الْعَظِيمِ **(129)**

« Hasbiya llaahou, laa ilaaha illa houwa,
aalayehi tawakkaltou, wa houwa rabbou
l-aarshi l-aadiimi.»

**"Allâh is sufficient for me. Lâ ilâha illa
Huwa (none has the right to be
worshipped but He) in Him I put my trust
and He is the Lord of the Mighty Throne. »**

Suah AL Ma'idah (Ayaa 83) : سورة المائدة

رَبَّنَا آَمَنَّا فَاكْتُبْنَا مَعَ الشَّاهِدِينَ

« Rabbanaa aamannaa, faketoubenaa
ma-aa shaahidiina »

**« Our Lord. We believe; so write us
down among the witnesses. »**

سورة القصص :Surah Al-Qasas

قَالَ رَبِّ إِنِّي ظَلَمْتُ نَفْسِي فَٱغْفِرْ لِي فَغَفَرَ لَهُۥٓ إِنَّهُۥ هُوَ ٱلْغَفُورُ ٱلرَّحِيمُ
(16)

« Qaala rabbi innii dalamtou nafsii faghfire lii, faghafara lahou innahou houwa lghafourou rrahiimou. »

« He said: My Lord. Verily, I have wronged myself, so forgive me.
Then He forgave him. Verily, He is the Oft-Forgiving, the Most Merciful. »

سورة القصص :**Surah Al-Qasas**

رَبِّ نَجِّنِي مِنَ الْقَوْمِ الظَّالِمِينَ (21)

« Rabbi najjinii mina lqawemi ddalimiina. »

« My Lord! Save me from the people who are wrong-doers (Zâlimûn) »

سورة القصص: **Surah Al-Qasas**

رَبِّ إِنِّي لِمَا أَنْزَلْتَ إِلَيَّ مِنْ خَيْرٍ فَقِيرٌ (24)

« Rabbi innii limaa anezalta ilayya mine
khayerine faqiirou. »

**« My Lord. truly, I am in need of whatever
good that You bestow on me. »**

الحمد لله ربي العالمين

"Alhamdou lilaahi rabbi l-aalamiine »

**Praise be to Allah, the Cherisher
and Sustainer of the worlds.**

Please, if you have any remark, contact us via
this e-mail: <u>apamog@hotmail.com</u>

Made in the USA
Las Vegas, NV
10 July 2024

92123847R00052